Canada's Bugs

Diane Swanson

Scholastic Canada Ltd.

Toronto New York London Auckland Sydney
Mexico City New Delhi Hong Kong Buenos Aires

Scholastic Canada Ltd.
604 King Street West, Toronto, Ontario M5V 1E1, Canada

Scholastic Inc.
557 Broadway, New York, NY 10012, USA

Scholastic Australia Pty Limited
PO Box 579, Gosford, NSW 2250, Australia

Scholastic New Zealand Limited
Private Bag 94407, Botany, Manukau 2163, New Zealand

Scholastic Children's Books
Euston House, 24 Eversholt Street, London NW1 1DB, UK

Library and Archives Canada Cataloguing in Publication
Swanson, Diane, 1944-
 Canada's bugs / Diane Swanson.
(Canada close up)
ISBN 978-0-439-94673-5
1. Insects--Canada--Juvenile literature. I. Title.
II. Series: Canada close up (Toronto, Ont.)
QL467.2.S963 2007   j595.70971   C2006-906730-9

Based on insect articles previously published in the "Bug Beat" in YES *Magazine*.

6 5 4 3 2   Printed in Canada   119   10 11 12 13

Chapter 1

ROBBER FLY

Grab, stab, poison and suck. A robber fly does not play with its prey. The fly holds the prey and spears it with a beaklike mouth. Next, the fly fills the prey with poison. This turns the prey's insides to liquid. Then, like drinking juice from a straw, the robber fly sucks the prey dry.

Robber flies hunt for their prey in fields and gardens. Many **species** have beardlike bristles on their faces. These bristles help protect their eyes from struggling prey. That is a good thing because robber flies are not afraid to attack larger insects, such as dragonflies.

Robber flies also prey on stinging insects, such as bees. If they have the chance, they even prey on other robber flies. Some scientists think that by eating so many different kinds of bugs, robber flies may help keep a balance in the insect world.

Robber flies are built for hunting. They have heads that can turn to watch for insects, strong wings to fly well and bristly legs to scoop up prey.

A robber fly usually zooms above its victim. Then it drops down, catching its prey in midair. But sometimes a fly is fooled by falling leaves or other things that float in the air. It might race from its perch, but then turn back when it sees that the moving object is not prey.

New robber flies hatch from eggs. They do not have wings, and look more like worms than flies. They are called **larvae**. Robber fly larvae usually live in soil or rotting wood. They feed on other insect larvae and bits of plants. It can take between one and three years for the larvae to become adults. But once they do, they are ready to terrorize the insect world!

Feats

Some robber flies copy other insects, such as bumblebees. The flies can even buzz. This may help fool anything that wants to eat the flies.

Robber flies can get really big. One of the largest species has a body — and a wingspan — of over 6 centimetres. It lives in South America.

There are about five thousand species of robber flies in the world. You can find about two hundred robber fly species in Canada.

Folklore

To people who lived about two hundred years ago, robber flies were a lot like highway robbers. Highway robbers were thieves on horseback who stole from travellers along the road. That is how the flies got their name. Like highway robbers, they would silently wait for their victims to pass by, then chase them down. Both kinds of robbers were swift and strong. But highway robbers stole money and jewellery. Robber flies stole lives.

Chapter 2

CLICK BEETLE

The click beetle got its name because it plays a terrific trick. When it is in danger, it pretends to be dead. It falls on its arched back with its legs curled. If this fools the animal hunting the beetle, the animal will give up and go away.

If that does not work, then the click beetle suddenly straightens its back. With a CLICK or SNAP, it jumps into the air. If it lands on its back, then the click beetle jumps again. The beetle keeps jumping until it lands on its feet. The sudden jumping and loud sounds often scare a hunter away. Even if they do not, the click beetle may have jumped far enough to run for safety!

Click beetles are born as larvae. Like other larvae, they look different from the adult insects. But these larvae are well named, too. They are called wireworms because they look like worms and their bodies are hard, like pieces of wire.

Wireworms prefer darkness to light. That is why they make their homes in dim places, such as soil and rotten wood. They might also crawl under tree bark.

In western Canada, farmers are not big fans of prairie grain wireworms. These wireworms eat their crops! Mother click beetles lay two hundred to four hundred eggs in the soil. When the larvae

hatch three to seven weeks later, they begin to eat roots and seeds. They attack different kinds of grasses, potatoes, corn, lettuce, sunflowers and onions.

It is hard to stop wireworms from eating farmers' crops. They are tough and survive winter by hibernating in the soil. It takes four to eleven years for the wireworms to grow up. But once they become click beetles, it is hard not to admire their high-flying leaps. CLICK!

Feats

About seven thousand to nine thousand species of click beetles live around the world.

Some click beetle larvae help save trees by eating the larvae of wood-boring beetles.

The spots on the back of a large-eyed click beetle look like big eyes. They help scare away animals that want to eat the beetle.

In some parts of the world, click beetles can be bioluminescent (bi-o-loo-muh-NESS-ent). This means that they can shine with a natural, heatless light.

Folklore

People used to believe that the bioluminescent light made by click beetles was magic. But they still put that light to good use. Some folks attached several click beetles to their heads so that the bugs' light would brighten dark paths. At fancy parties, women decorated their hair and dresses with shining click beetles.

Chapter 3

EARWIG

Lots of things "go in one ear and out the other," but an earwig is not one of them. An earwig searches for small, shady spaces. So there is a small chance one might crawl into your ear if you were outside sleeping. But it is unlikely. Despite its name, an earwig has no interest in ears. Instead, it crawls under stones or hides in tree bark.

Earwigs also have large pincers on their back ends. These are called cerci. But you do not have to worry about them either. The cerci [SIR-sie] can deliver a pinch, but it is often too weak for humans to feel. The earwigs use their cerci to scare away insects, spiders and small birds who want to eat them. If they need to, earwigs can also use their cerci to wound attackers. Some kinds of earwigs squirt a bad-smelling liquid at their enemies.

Earwigs grow by **moulting**. This means that they outgrow their outer covering and shed it. Most earwigs moult four to six times before they become adults. Some adult earwigs have two pairs of wings. One pair is small and thick. The other pair is large and thin and shaped like ears. The small wings protect the large, folded ones until they open for flight. Earwig wings are not very strong, so the insects rarely fly. Instead, they scurry around on their six legs. They mostly feed on dead or decaying plants and different kinds of insect larvae.

Even without flying, earwigs have managed to travel the world. They have tucked themselves inside luggage, food cartons and crates. One toured the international postal system inside a letter! Of course, earwigs do not plan these trips. They just happen to settle into the cracks of things that get moved around a lot. Most of the earwigs found in Canada are European earwigs. They likely came here by accident, too — just by being in the wrong place at the wrong time!

Feats

Sometimes hundreds of earwigs group together beneath a single rock.

Earwigs are always on guard. They keep their antennae in touch with their surroundings while they rest.

When it hatches, an earwig uses a special "tooth" to break out of its egg.

Some female earwigs make surprisingly good moms. They are one of the few kinds of insects that clean and protect the eggs they lay. They even care for their just-hatched young, which are called **nymphs**.

Folklore

The earwig has scared people in many parts of the world. Some folks believed it could wriggle its way through their ears and into their brain. Other people blamed the insect for their loss of hearing. They tried to cure themselves with a mixture of dried earwigs and hare urine!

Chapter 4

FIREFLY

FLASH . . . flash, flash . . . FLASH. The tiny lights of the firefly send out a message: "Hey, I'm over here. I'm female. I'm ready to mate."

In the night sky, a male firefly sees the flashes. Their pattern can tell him if he and the female are the same species. If they are, he flashes a message back: "Message received. I'm coming!" The partners repeat their messages until the male reaches the female and they mate.

Not all species of fireflies twinkle, but many do. This is because they are bioluminescent. When certain chemicals mix inside them, the mixture creates light energy. Unlike most light bulbs, the light energy that fireflies make is almost heat-free. In many species, the light-making organs sit near the end of their bodies, like tail lights on cars.

In some species the female fireflies are wingless and cannot fly. Some people call them glow-worms. Instead of flying, they twist their bodies around to send their messages in different directions. Some of them also send false signals. They lure the males of different species and then eat them!

Even firefly larvae glow. They are also called glow-worms. Scientists think the larvae might use their tail lights to send out a warning: "Yucky tasting. Do not eat."

The larvae live in soil, rotten wood or leaf litter. They eat worms, snails and slugs. When the larvae are about two years old, each one builds a dirt ball around its body. A week or two later, they come out of their dirt balls as adult fireflies.

Most adults live less than three weeks. Although some of them feed, many of them do not. But they all try to mate, and that is when you see their amazing light show! Flash . . . Flash . . .

Feats

🪲 Firefly larvae track down snails and slugs by following their trails of slime.

🪲 Some tropical fireflies flash in huge masses.

🪲 While Canada has some species of fireflies that do not make any light, most do. You can see their lights flickering over fields on warm summer nights.

🪲 Fireflies are sometimes called lightning bugs. And did you know that they are not flies at all? They are actually beetles!

Folklore

Are fireflies a good sign or a bad one?
It depends on where you live!

✳ In Europe a firefly inside a house is thought to be a sign that someone will die soon.

✳ In Japan fireflies are blessed as the spirits of soldiers who have died for their country.

✳ In some Mediterranean countries, the flashing of fireflies is feared. The light is thought to come from graves.

✳ In North America a glow-worm on a path signals success.

Chapter 5

FLEA

Fleeing a flea can be hard! Oh sure, it is just a tiny bug (often less than 4 millimetres long). And it does not have wings, so it cannot fly. But a flea is a great jumper!

Using its strong back legs, it can leap about 60 centimetres. It can jump either upward or sideways. That is how it gets on its victims to draw their blood.

Fleas have been around for millions of years. Imagine them leaping onto prehistoric animals, piercing their skin with sharp mouthparts and sucking up blood. Today, fleas feed on animals such as rabbits, squirrels, cats and dogs. They even feed on people. Some also suck blood from birds, such as chickens.

Depending on the species, a flea might stay on its animal host or just show up at dinnertime. Its antennae and bristles can tell when a host is close by. It can sense the body heat of the animal, the air it breathes out and its movement.

Fleas are made to travel through the coats of other animals. Their bodies are flat on either side. This makes it easy for them to slip through fur and feathers. Bristles help them cling to these coats.

Some fleas are able to feed, without stopping, for four hours. They take in much more blood than

they need. The extra bit squirts out of their rear ends. It often falls where their host rests. There, flea larvae feed on the specks of blood. It is an important part of their meals until they grow and spin their cocoons. When they come out of their cocoons, they are adult fleas. They are ready to hunt for fresh blood!

Feats

🦟 Different species of fleas can feed on a single animal — all at the same time.

🦟 If you let your dog or cat outside in August, September or October, you might find they pick up more fleas. In Canada those are the best months for fleas to survive outdoors.

🦟 Some flea eggs can hatch in a day.

🦟 A flea can live several months without food.

🦟 Even fleas that have been frozen for a year have survived.

🦟 Fleas can be hosts, too. Sometimes small mites fit between the plates in the flea's hard covering and go along for a ride.

🦟 Did you know that flea circuses used to be popular? The fleas did tricks, and could pull objects as heavy to them as an elephant would be to you!

Folklore

✴ It was once believed that fleas only attacked lazy people.

✴ Some people used to believe that if you caught a single flea in March, then you could get rid of another hundred.

✴ Ancient Romans thought that fleas were caused by sunlight hitting dirt and grime.

Chapter 6

GRASSHOPPER

Even an Olympic athlete would be jealous of a grasshopper. It can jump distances fifteen to twenty times its own length! But grasshoppers are made to jump. Their two back legs are long and powerful. The top parts of these legs have thick muscles. In fact, their back legs are so perfect for jumping that grasshoppers are clumsy walkers.

When a grasshopper gets ready to hop, its four smaller legs push up the front part of its body. Its back legs suddenly shoot out. The grasshopper is fired into the air. It leaps from spot to spot. It can travel up to ten times faster by leaping than most other insects can by running.

There are more than five thousand species of grasshoppers in the world. Many of them can fly as well as jump. They have a pair of thick front wings and a pair of filmy back wings. When grasshoppers fly, they hold their front wings out and beat their back ones. But even if they have wings, grasshoppers still travel more often by jumping than by flying.

Some grasshopper species use their wings to create music. Male grasshoppers use their music to attract mates and to tell other males to get lost. How they make their music depends on their species. Some grasshoppers do it by scraping tiny pegs on their back legs against their front wings. Others rub these wings against each other. In flight, some

species hit their back legs with their wings to make noise. Some just snap their wings together.

To hear all this music, some grasshoppers have eardrums just below their wings on either side of their bodies. Others have eardrums in their front legs. Listening helps females tell whether or not the musicians are likely mates. That's because each species makes its own special song.

Feats

Millions of grasshoppers have flown together in a single group called a swarm. The swarm was so thick it blocked out the sunlight.

The world's largest grasshoppers are about 150 millimetres long. The smallest measure less than 6 millimetres.

Grasshoppers cannot drink. They get their water from the plants they eat.

A female grasshopper can dig a burrow using the tiny hooks she has on her rear end. Then she lays twenty to a hundred eggs in the burrow.

The differential grasshopper, found throughout Canada, can eat sixteen times its weight in food in a day.

Folklore

✳ When you catch a grasshopper, it might try to protect itself by oozing drops of a brown, bad-tasting liquid. Some people believe this liquid gets rid of warts.

✳ Some Asian tales describe the grasshopper as a combination of seven animals. They claim it has the head of a horse, the neck of an ox, the wings of a dragon, the horns of a stag, the body of a scorpion, the feet of a camel and the tail of a serpent.

Chapter 7

HONEYBEE

She loops this way. She loops that way. She waggles side to side and dances while she hums. She is a honeybee. Her movements tell other bees that she has found a good source of flower nectar and pollen. Her dance can even tell them where to find it.

Honeybees live in groups called colonies. A colony is made up of thousands of bees. Their home is known as a hive. It has a single queen bee. Her only job is to lay eggs — up to 1500 a day! She has no time to do anything else, so she is cared for by female honeybees called workers.

Just as their name says, worker bees do all the work around the colony. They build combs of wax, clean house, find food and care for the larvae and the queen. They also defend the colony with their stingers.

Once the bees have stung something, their stingers are pulled from their bodies. This kills them.

Worker bees gather pollen and nectar from many different plants. They carry the pollen in baskets formed by hair on their back legs. The nectar is carried in special stomachs called crops.

Back home, the bees put the nectar into cells. They make honey by beating their wings over it. This evaporates the water in the nectar, which means that the water turns into a gas and becomes part of the air. When most of the water is gone, the nectar becomes honey.

If a queen dies, the workers replace her. They move a fresh egg to a large cell. When a larva comes out of the egg, they raise it to be their new queen. They do this by feeding it royal jelly, which is a mixture of honey, pollen and a special liquid that comes from the bees.

Drones, or male bees, mate with the new queen, then die. But the queen has what she needs to lay more eggs. Life in the colony goes on.

Feats

In a single day, a honeybee might travel 16 kilometres to gather nectar and pollen for her hive.

To make half a kilogram of honey, bees have to visit about two million flowers.

Honeybees beat their wings about two hundred times per second.

There are almost nine thousand beekeepers in Canada.

Canadians love their honey. But bees are also important to us because they help to pollinate so many of our crops.

Folklore

✳ It was once believed that fighting among a human family would drive honeybees away from a hive.

✳ A baby whose lips were touched by a honeybee was supposed to become a great speaker or storyteller.

✳ Some people in the United States used to believe that bad luck followed anyone who ate honey or used wax made by an enemy's bees.

✳ Feeling down or upset? Some people think honey can make you feel better.

Chapter 8

HORSEFLY

They are tough and out for blood! Female horseflies often feed on blood. They suck it from your dog, your horse, your cow – even you! They slice through skin with sharp mouthparts that are built like razors. They can suck for minutes at a time.

Horseflies pump their spit into the bite. This keeps the blood flowing. Do not worry: one or two flies cannot take enough blood to harm you. But their bites do hurt. And their spit can cause an allergic reaction. If you are outside and want to keep the horseflies away, try wearing light-coloured clothes and stay in the shade.

Both male and female horseflies are powerful, two-winged fliers. For fuel, they drink nectar and other plant juices. Only the females drink blood. All day, the horseflies zoom about, looking for food. Sometimes they look for mates, too.

Once they have mated, female horseflies lay their eggs in clumps. They usually lay them on plants near water. They make a waterproof ooze and use it to cover the eggs. That helps hold the eggs together.

A few days later, the larvae hatch. They often burrow into damp soil close to marshes, rivers and lakes. They eat what ever is handy, such as tiny

critters and rotting plants. How much time the horseflies spend as larvae depends on the species and where they live. It might be up to three years.

When they are ready, the horsefly larvae head to drier spots. They stop eating and moving. They become **pupae**. This means that they develop cases around their bodies. Inside their cases, the larvae turn into grown adult flies. This can take twelve days. When they come out of the cases, they are hungry and ready to eat. So watch out for those female horseflies!

Feats

Adult horseflies have huge heads and thick bodies. They can be more than 25 millimetres long.

A horsefly can fly at speeds of 25 kilometres per hour.

There are seventy-five species of horseflies in Canada.

One female horsefly can lay up to one thousand eggs at a time.

The larva of a horsefly can pull its head right into its body.

Horsefly larvae are cannibals. This means that they eat other horsefly larvae.

Folklore

✳ In North America some folks believed that a powerful spirit punished a tribe that was too lazy to grow food for winter. The spirit turned the tribe into flies that ate garbage, such as rotting fruit and vegetables.

✳ In South America, horseflies were thought to be dead chiefs who came to take away the souls of dying relatives.

✳ In Scotland, some people thought it was a sign of good luck to have a fly drop into a glass just as a drinker started to sip.

Chapter 9

LADYBUG

Take your pick: ladybug, ladybird, lady beetle, ladyfly, even ladycow. Whatever you call it, this little bug is still a beetle. It has beetle wing covers and biting mouthparts. The bug was named after Our Lady, the Virgin Mary. This is because people in Europe once believed that the bug could perform miracles, such as saving farm crops from ruin.

But a ladybug cannot perform miracles. It just eats lots of insects called aphids, which eat crops.

Even a ladybug larva is a powerful eating machine. A large larva can wolf down five hundred plant-sucking aphids in a day. This has earned the larva a nickname: aphid wolf. Lucky for the ladybug larva, aphids are slow. The larva can take its time feeding. It wanders around plants where aphids hang out, and chomps up whatever it bumps into.

If an adult ladybug has trouble finding aphids, it can do without food for a while. Sometimes it feeds on flower pollen. In emergencies it might eat its own larvae and eggs.

People often find a ladybug's bold colours and patterns pretty. But these colours and patterns turn off many insect-eating animals. The colours warn: "I stink, and I taste yucky, too." If that warning does not work, the ladybug squirts a foul-tasting yellow blood from its legs. It even plays dead. It falls on its back with all six legs and both antennae held close to its body. When danger has passed, the ladybug presses down with its wing covers and flips itself right side up.

There are about 160 ladybug species in Canada. Years ago people brought multicoloured Asian lady beetles over from Asia to help eat aphids. Now they can be seen all over Canada. These yellow and orange ladybugs sometimes bite if you try to hold them. It does not hurt, but it is not what you would expect from ladybugs!

Feats

Ladybugs can walk upside down. They have sticky pads on the end of their legs.

There are thousands of species of ladybugs in the world. They have different patterns, and can be different colours, including green and yellow.

Some ladybugs hibernate in huge groups. High in the Sierra Nevada, a mountain range in California, scientists once found crowds of ladybugs that covered areas as big as four football fields.

Twelve hungry ladybugs might be all you need to clean up the aphids on an infested fruit tree.

Folklore

✳ In some parts of the world, people believed ladybugs could cure them of illnesses such as measles.

✳ Got a toothache? A while ago, some people might have told you to stuff a crushed ladybug into a tooth cavity.

✳ A ladybug walking across the hand of a woman was thought to be a sign she would soon marry.

✳ Good luck and good weather arrive with ladybugs — if you believe these insects have special powers.

Chapter 10

MOSQUITO

They buzz your ears. They bite your skin. They leave you scratching for days. Mosquitoes are annoying, but they are also amazing. Female mosquitoes can lay one hundred to four hundred eggs at a time. In hot weather it can take just four days for mosquitoes to hatch and become adults. Even in cooler weather it can take only one or two weeks.

Some mosquitoes lay their eggs on moist soil. Some lay them on rocks and plants that will soon be covered by water. Others deposit their eggs in or on the water and glue them together.

Mosquito larvae have big heads and long antennae, but no legs. They grow in water, where they swim quickly by throwing their bodies from side to side. That is why they are sometimes called "wigglers." Most mosquito larvae eat micro-organisms, which are tiny living things such as bacteria. They also eat bits of plants. The larvae gather their food using brushes of hair near their mouths. The brushes trap the food. They can also make water currents that draw food toward the mouth. As the larvae feed, they grow fast. They moult four times before they change into pupae.

Mosquito pupae are called "tumblers." Unlike other kinds of pupae, they can be very active. They do not eat, but they swim fast when

disturbed. They usually head to the bottom of the water and hide.

As adults, male mosquitoes use their antennae to hear the hum of females in flight. That is how they find their mates. Once they have mated, the females search for blood meals to help their eggs develop. When a female mosquito finds a host, she cuts through its skin, injects her spit to keep the blood flowing, then pumps blood out. She eats until she nearly bursts. She often doubles her weight in a single meal. It is her spit that makes her bite mark itchy. If you are lucky, you will not be her next meal!

Feats

There are more than three thousand species of mosquitoes in the world. There are about seventy-five different species in Canada.

A mosquito can beat its wings six hundred times a second.

Just one meal of blood can nourish one hundred mosquito eggs.

Some pitcher plant mosquito larvae spend the winter in ice — the frozen water held by pitcher plants.

Folklore

Where do mosquitoes come from?

✳ In northern Japan there is a legend about a one-eyed, bear-like goblin that ate people. A hunter killed the goblin and set its body on fire. The ashes turned into biting insects, including mosquitoes.

✳ In eastern Canada a legend tells of a spirit that turned dirt on clothes into mosquitoes. The spirit was punishing a woman for being too lazy to clean her husband's clothes.

Glossary

Larvae [LARH-vie] Many insects are born as larvae. They are wingless at this stage, which is known as the feeding stage. To become adult insects, they undergo a complete metamorphosis [met-uh-MORE-fuh-sis] or change. From larvae, they become **pupae** [PYOO-pie]. Most insects in this stage do not feed or move. Their bodies are changing. Some are in cocoons. After the pupal stage, they will be adult insects.

Moulting Many insects moult, which means that they outgrow their outer coverings and cast them off. They grow new coverings to replace the old.

Nymphs [nimfz] Some insects do not have a pupal stage. They are born as nymphs and only change slightly to become adult insects.

Species [SPEE-seez] A species is one kind or group of living things. Members of the same species can mate and produce young that can also mate. For example, tigers and jaguars are two different species of cat.